QUOTES ILLUSTRATED

100 WORKS OF ART INSPIRED BY WORDS
LESLEY RILEY

ARTIST
SUCCESS
PRESS

Artist Success Press
Frederick, MD

ISBN:0615918557
ISBN-13: 978-0615918556
1. Art -Mixed media 2. Quotations

This book was created for and is dedicated to everyone who wishes to be inspired.

The Story Behind This Book

Lesley Riley

My first introduction to quotes was my father's well-worn, blue hardback copy of Bartlett's Familiar Quotations. I remember it being quite heavy for my 10 year old hands – a large book with tiny print that filled every inch on every page. This book was full of amazing insight and wisdom. I understood the magic it held even at that early age.

Quotes became a visual obsession a few years later when the Abbey Press catalog arrived in our mailbox full of brightly colored 60s era illustrated quotes by Sister Corita Kent and others. It was the first place I read the words that set me on my path to becoming an artist:

"Whatever you do, or dream you can, begin it.
Boldness has genius and power
and magic in it."
Goethe

I have been collecting quotes for over 40 years. Thankfully it's much easier now with word processors, internet quote sites and search engines. But I still love to pull my very 1970s colored journal off the shelf, smile at my teenage penmanship, and read over the words that inspired and influenced me back then.

Today, finding a quote takes nothing more than a visit to Google to type in the few words of a quote I am looking for. That is, if it's not already in my vast collection. I have a two-column, 126 page WORD document that right now contains 41,657 words of wisdom. By the time you read this, I know there will be more. I add to it daily.

You see, I'm fascinated by how much I glean from these bite-sized thoughts of famous and not-so or not-even famous people that have been preserved for posterity. I call it my *quotespiration*.

Back in 1989, I tucked Goethe's quote in that whisper of space between the frame and the mirror so that I would see it every day. *"Whatever you do, or dream you can, begin it."* Begin it...begin it... It took me several years to work up the courage to begin it. Ten to be exact. And I can tell you now, 25 years later, that it's so true, so powerfully true. Boldness *does* have "genius and power and magic in it."

As a quote collector, one of the things that fascinates me is how often you will hear the same wisdom or knowledge shared again and again by so many different people over time – even centuries. They endure perhaps in part by being short and concise - most quotes are less than three sentences. Marcus Tullius Cicero

(106 BC-43 BC), who preserved many ancient quotes with his writings, said "Brevity is a great charm of eloquence."

I believe quotes are powerful. They are moments of wisdom, insight and truth which inspire, guide and remind. They speak of what we know but haven't been paying attention to and make us want to pay attention.

In his book, *Quotology*, Willis Goth Regier says, "Oh to say something so fine, so memorable, that it carries across time, oceans, and languages...as if a few sentences, or one alone, could touch hearts, grasp truth, and endure." So many quotes have touched my heart and stayed with me for decades. They are a part of me and their words of wisdom have formed who I am today.

What you now hold in your hands is the culmination of a dream. It is a combination of the two things that I carry in my heart and soul as guiding lights - quotes and art. It is my attempt at the ultimate in inspiration - words and works of art that will move you to smile, to feel happy and think positively. But most of all, I hope to inspire you to take action on your dreams.

This book is a result of the friendship and community I have found by taking action on my own dreams and following my passion. It would not be anywhere near as expressive and rich without the many artists who responded to my call for art. I assigned the quotes that inspired their creations, but many also chose a quote of their own, or even quoted themselves.

My seed of an idea became a rich community garden of delight thanks to their contributions. This book would not exist without their time and talent. I want to thank you, too, for sharing this experience with me.

Lesley Riley

Lesley Riley

To be that self which one truly is.
Søren Kierkegaard

It doesn't happen all at once.
You become. It takes a long time.
Margery Williams

Sharon Hendry

drawing: watercolor, pen & ink

Inside the image, the quote on the photograph reads:

I found God
in myself
& I loved her
fiercely.

— Ntozáke Shange

i found god in myself and i loved her i loved her fiercely
Ntozake Shange

Shimoda

quilt: fabric, appliqué, hand and machine stitched

The color of springtime is in the flowers; the color of winter is in the imagination.
Terri Guillemets

Karen O'Brien

collage: painting, drawing, acrylic, watercolor, pencil

Ring the bells that still can ring
Forget your perfect offering
There is a crack in everything
That's how the light gets in.
Leonard Cohen

Linda Teddlie Minton

original digital collage: painting, ink, hand & machine stitched

I don't want to be a passenger in my own life.
Diane Ackerman

Liz Thoresen

painting: pastel, PanPastel, pastel pencils, collage

Stay firmly in your path and dare; be wild two hours a day!
Paul Gauguin

Liz Kettle

collage: paint, paper

We are cups, constantly and quietly being filled.

The trick is knowing

how to tip ourselves over and let the

beautiful stuff out.
Ray Bradbury

We're cups constantly and quietly being filled. The trick is knowing
how to tip ourselves over and let the beautiful stuff out.
Ray Bradbury

Judy Coates Perez

painted fabric collage: rubber stamps, printed tissue-tex, free motion stitching

You never have to change anything you got up in the middle of the night to write.
Saul Bellow

Theresa Wells Stifel

collage: stitching, embroidery, acrylic paint, fabric, paper

No trumpets sound when the important decisions of our life are made.
Destiny is made known silently.
Agnes De Mille

Kirsten Varga

painting: collage, acrylic paint, paper, crackle medium

Some days there won't be a song in your heart. Sing anyway.
Emory Austin

Meena Schaldenbrand

quilt: fabric, machine appliqué and quilting, embellishments

Art offers sanctuary to everyone willing to open their hearts as well as their eyes.
Nikki Giovanni

Kirsten Varga

painting: crackle medium, acrylic paint, transfers, alcohol inks, paint pen

Beauty is the sense of life and the awe one has in its presence.
Willa Cather

Pearl Red Moon

fiber collage: fabric, acrylic paint, embroidery, felting fibers

And above all, watch with glittering eyes the whole world around you because the greatest secrets are always hidden in the most unlikely places. Those who don't believe in magic will never find it.
Roald Dahl

Gina Louthian-Stanley

mixed-media collage: digital collage, vintage photograph, painting

As the sun makes it new
Day by day make it new
Yet again make it new.
Ezra Pound's Confucian translation

Jill K. Berry

mixed media on wood: painting, calligraphy, copper carving, stone inlay

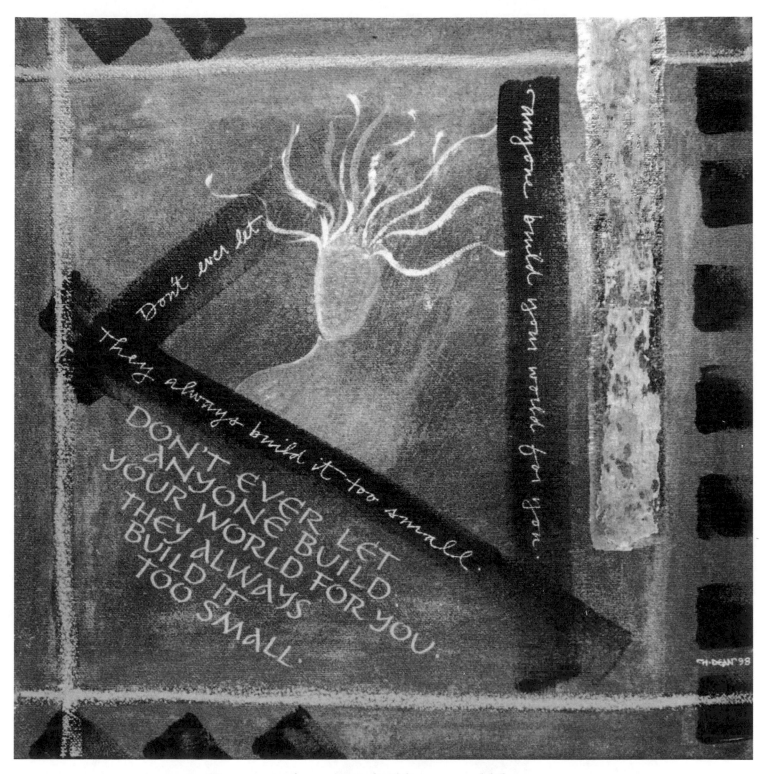

Don't ever let anyone build your world for you.
They always build it too small.
Holly Dean

Holly Dean

painting: calligraphy, faux guilding, patinas

Art to me was a state; it didn't need to be an accomplishment.
Margaret Anderson

Dawn Collins

layered mixed media painting

We tend not to choose the unknown and yet it is the unknown
with all its disappointments and surprises that is the most enriching.
Anne Morrow Lindberg

Tricia Scott

painting: drawing, acrylic, graphite

If the angel deigns to come it will be because you have convinced her,
not by tears but by your humble resolve to be always beginning; to be a beginner.
Ranier Maria Rilke

Jennifer Johns

oil painting on canvas board

The soul should always stand ajar, ready to welcome ecstatic experience.
Emily Dickinson

Silvia Souza

digital collage

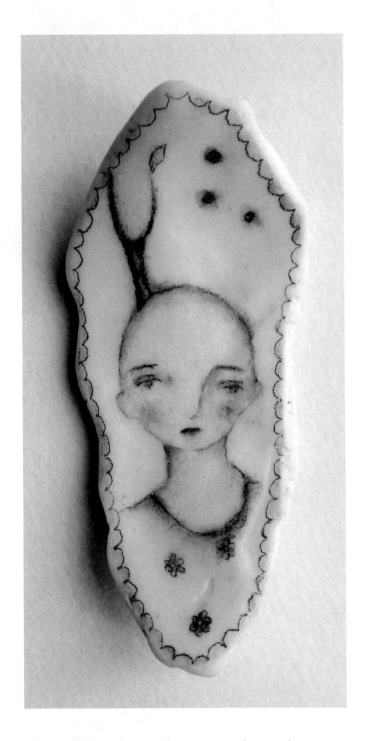

At the center of your being you have the answer;
you know who you are and you know what you want.
Lao Tzu

Lynne Hoppe

drawing: colored pencil, cold wax, shell

When I gaze upon your face I envision a story of quiet strength and I'm encouraged
to create a story through fabric. When I gaze upon you, I see beauty.
'Lovey' Lavette Johnson-Debrow

'Lovey' Lavette Johnson-Debrow

fabric photo collage: machine stitched

They say that times changes things, but you actually have to change them yourself.
Andy Warhol

Sarah Cooper

mixed media collage: painting

We are so many selves...the person we were last year, wanted to be yesterday, tried to become in one job or in one winter, in one love affair or even in one house where even now, we can close our eyes and smell the rooms.
Gloria Steinem

Marcia Beckett

painting: watercolor, acrylic paint, markers, scratching

She had found a jewel down inside herself and she had wanted to walk
where people could see her and gleam it around.
Zora Neal Hurston

Sandy Lupton

painting: deconstructed screen print, drawing, collage

Be quite still and solitary. The world will freely offer itself to you unmasked.
It has no choice. It will roll in ecstasy at your feet.
Franz Kafka

Seth Apter

book cover collage: photograph paper, ink, wax pastel, crayon, lettering

It isn't the great big pleasures that count the most, it's making a great deal out of the little ones.
Jean Webster

Deborah Guthrie

collage: painting, drawing, glazing

Life is a spell so exquisite that everything conspires to break it.
Emily Dickinson

Paula Guerin

collage and painting on wrapped canvas

We have a tendency to obscure the forest of simple joys with the trees of problems.
Christine Collange

Linda H. MacDonald

quilt: appliqué, thread painting, machine quilting

We grow neither better nor worse as we get old, but more like ourselves.
May Lamberton Becker

Paula Guerin

collage and paint on wrapped canvas

There was never a place for her in the ranks of the terrible, slow
army of the cautious. She ran ahead where there were no paths.
Dorothy Parker

Joanie Springer

painting: gouache, paper mounted on wood panel

Perfection is achieved, not when there is nothing more to add,
but when there is nothing left to take away.
Antoine de Saint Exupéry

Joyce L. Carrier

quilt: fabric, cutaway, hand-dyed silk, rayon, thread, cording, free motion stitching, bobbin work

Each thing she learned became a part of herself to be used
over and over in new adventures.
Kate Seredy

Ellen Wilson

collage: stamping, stitching, paper, embellishments

Nonsense and beauty have close connections.
E. M. Forster

Sandy Lupton

collage: painting, deconstructed screen print, drawing

We are always the same age inside.
Gertrude Stein

Kim Tedrow

collage: watercolor, acrylic paint, paper, stencil

The well of Providence is deep. It's the buckets we bring to it that are small.
Mary Webb

Catherine Martin

quilt: cotton, painted background, machine pieced, free motion quilting

In life as in dance: Grace glides on blistered feet.
Alice Abrams

Cheryl Stevenson

watercolor

I must be a mermaid. I have no fear of depths and a great fear of shallow living.
Anaïs Nin

Mindy Lacefield

digital and mixed media collage: paint, pencil

The object isn't to make art, it's to be in that
wonderful state which makes art inevitable.
Robert Henri

Rachel Stewart

assemblage: newspaper, stickers, found objects, paper, acrylic paint, beads

I decided to start anew, to strip away what I had been taught, to accept
as true my own thinking. This was one of the best times in my life.
Georgia O'Keefe

Dawn Collins

layered mixed media painting, Zentangle

Swimming upstream and lovin' it.
Bonnie J. Smith

Bonnie J. Smith

quilt: appliqué, cotton, wool, photo transfer, fusing, machine quilting

When we look at art we are looking for ourselves.
Lesley Riley

Susie Monday

quilt: fabric, screen printed, dyed, fused, machine and hand stitched

The muses love the morning.
Benjamin Franklin

Larkin Jean Van Horn

hand embroidery & beading: hand-painted cotton, tulle, machine stitching, glass beads, Swarovski crystals,
ceramic face by Diane Briegleb

Conditions for creativity are to be puzzled; to concentrate; to accept
conflict and tension; to be born everyday; to feel a sense of self.
Erich Fromm

Chris Cozen

digital collage: personal artwork

I want to remain in the open, becoming something
other than human under the sky.
Kathleen Norris

Doris Arndt

watercolor: hand lettering, salt resist, ink, colored pencil, silk flowers

Whatever you can do or dream you can, begin it.
Boldness has genius, magic and power in it.
Goethe

Carol Alt

collage: vintage papers, paint

The fragrance always remains in the hand that gives the rose.
Mahatma Ghandi

Vicki Szamborski

painting: drawing, collage stenciling, writing, acrylic paint, tissue paper, ink, pen

Woman in harmony with her spirit is like a river flowing. She goes where she will without pretense and arrives at her destination prepared to be herself and only herself.
Maya Angelou

Sandra Ahlgren Sapienza

handcut multi-layered stenciling: acrylic paint

The heart that breaks open can contain the whole universe.
Joanna Macy

Ingrid Dijkers

art journal: collage and painting

You've got to jump off cliffs all the time and build your wings on the way down.
Ray Bradbury

Stacey Merrill

mixed media: draw, paint, stamp, digital manipulation

It takes a lot of courage to show your dreams to someone else.
Erma Bombeck

Nanette Zeller

quilt: thread painting, appliqué, cotton, wool, hand-dyeds, machine quilting

Do not try to do extraordinary things, but do ordinary things with intensity.
Emily Carr

Sue Bellone Perna

paper maché: paper twisting, foil, metal findings

For my part I know nothing with any certainty
but the sight of the stars makes me dream.
Vincent Van Gogh

Jenny Rodda

watercolor: acrylic, ink, stamping, collage

The past is the beginning of the beginning and all
that is and has been is but the twilight of the dawn.
H. G. Wells

Michelle Tompkins

collage: sketching, painting, acrylic paint, water-soluble crayon

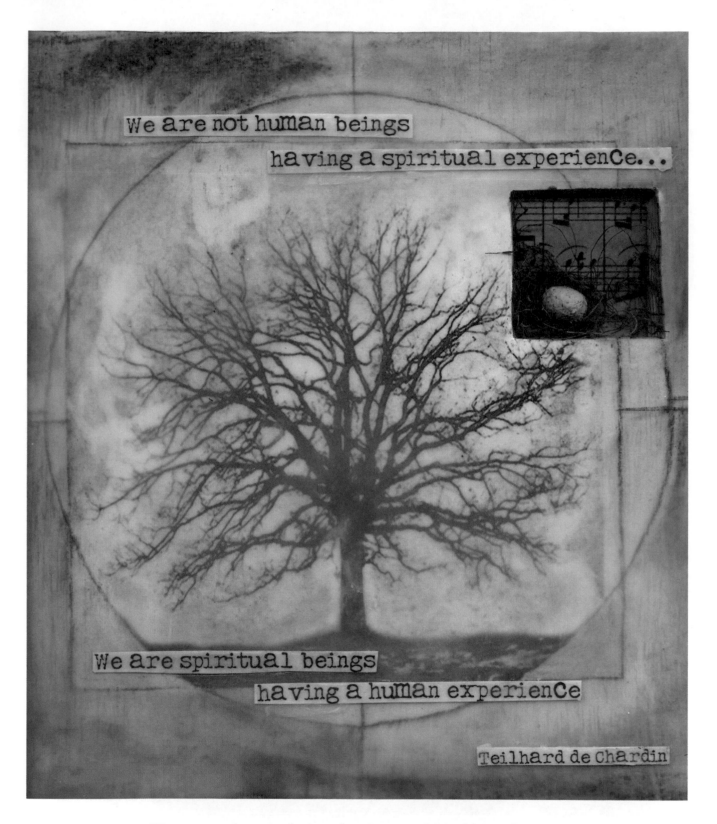

We are not human beings having a spiritual experience.
We are spiritual beings having a human experience.
Teilhard de Chardin

Patti Monroe-Mohrenweiser

encaustic painting: image transfer, graphite, drawing

Free your heart. Travel like the moon among the stars.
Buddha

Kim Ward

assemblage: painting, drawing, acrylics, colored pencil, found objects, crystals

Life begets energy. Energy creates energy. It is by spending oneself that we become rich.
Sarah Bernhardt

Sarah Cooper

mixed media collage: painting

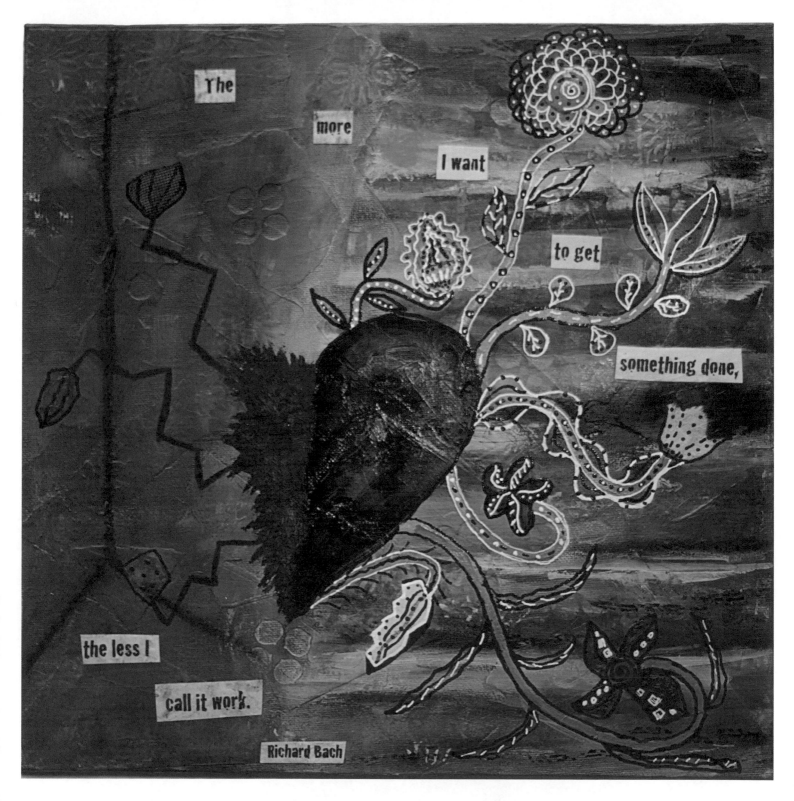

The more I want to get something done, the less I call it work.
Richard Bach

Linda C. Bannan

mixed media collage: acrylic paint, textured paper, dimensional pens

The breeze at dawn has secrets to tell you, don't go back to sleep.
Rumi

Theresa Martin

digital collage

I put on my dream-cap one day and stepped into Wonderland.
Howard Pyle

Catherine Anderson

digital photo collage: vintage papers, found images

Even if I knew that tomorrow the world would go to pieces,
I would still plant my apple tree.
Martin Luther King, Jr.

Jan Avellana

digital illustration

Grace must find expression in life, otherwise it is not grace.
Karl Barth

Carol Sloan

painting: plaster gauze, joint compound, canvas, carving, acrylic paint, glazes, driftwood

Only one thing has to change for us to know happiness in our lives:
where we focus our attention.
Greg Anderson

Barb Ingersoll

acrylic & watercolor painting on fabric: machine stitched and embellished

Bury doubt under wonder.
Ruth Radlauer

Tamara Tolkin

digital collage

The revelation was a little like what saints receive on
mountains - a further chapter in the history of the mystery.
Diane Ackerman

Leslie Levenson

digital collage: photography, watercolor

To dream of the person you would like
to be is to waste the person you are.
Sholem Asch

Marlynn Likens

fabric collage: embelishments

Art is not a handicraft, it is the transmission of feeling the artist has experienced.
Leo Tolstoy

Patricia J. Mosca

illustration: acrylic, watercolor paper

Tell me and I'll forget. Show me and I may not remember.
Involve me and I'll understand.
Native American Proverb

Carol Clarkson

wheel-thrown & hand-built altered clay: glazed

Thousands of things go right for you every day.
Rob Brezsny

Lucy Pearce Hughes

wet felting: needle felting, wool

Action in the face of uncertainty is essential to creation.
Jonathan Fields

Andrea Hawkes

collage: watercolor on rice paper

It always seems impossible until it's done.
Nelson Mandela

Darlene Campbell

watercolor

Art washes away from the soul the dust of everyday life.
Picasso

Cheryl Greenstreet

painted canvas: markers, mounted on silk over primed MDF

You may run, walk, stumble, drive or fly, but let us never lose sight
of the reason for the journey, or miss a chance to see a rainbow on the way.
Gloria Gaither

Deborah Guthrie

collage: painting, drawing, glazing

Kindness in words creates confidence.
Kindness in thinking creates profoundness.
Kindness in giving creates love.
Lao-Tze

Norina Morris

painting: acrylic, ink

I love even the smallest thing of all and I paint it on a golden background
and make it visible in order that it moves someone even if I don't know whom.
Ranier Maria Rilke

Serena Barton

painting: oil, cold wax

Normal is not something to aspire to, it is something to get away from.
Jodie Foster

Ruth Krening

collage: book spines, vintage ephemera

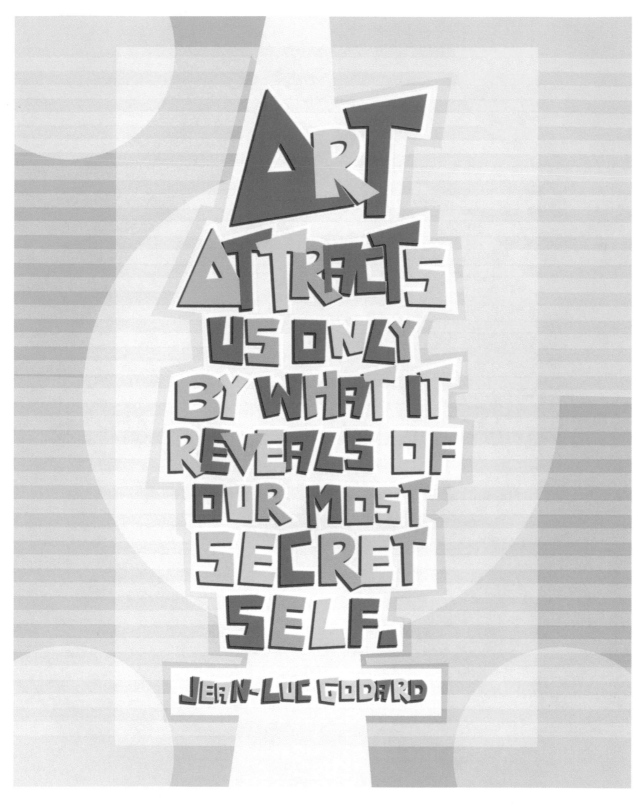

Art attracts us only by what it reveals of our most secret self.
Jean-Luc Goddard

Jerry Gonzalez

digital art

It may be hard for an egg to turn into a bird: it would be a jolly sight to fly
while remaining an egg. We are like eggs at present. And you cannot go on
indefinitely being just an ordinary decent egg. You must be hatched or go bad.
C. S. Lewis

Gina Armfield

watercolor

Toss in a stone and begin your own ripple of influence.
Joy Cooper

Stephanie Estrin

acrylic painting

If knowledge is power, then wisdom is humility.
Tico Colada

Tico Colada

quilt: appliqué, hand & machine embroidery, beading, polymer clay stamping

You are what you are when nobody is looking.
Abigail Van Buren

Cathy Bakke Martin

mixed media painting

Artists can color the sky red because they know that it is blue.
Jules Feiffer

Stacey Merrill

mixed media: drawing, painting, digital manipulation

The aim of art is to represent not the outward
appearance of things but their inward significance.
Aristotle

Adeola Davies-Aiyeloja

mixed media painting on paper

The most beautiful things in the world cannot be seen
or even touched. They must be felt with the heart.
Helen Keller

Lucy Landry

doll: felt, wool, hand-dyed cotton, needle felting, hand-embroidery, beading

Let a joy keep you. Reach out your hands and take it when it runs by.
Carl Sandburg

Lisa K. Chin

monoprinted fabric: handmade & commercial stencils, acrylic paint, thread

All the art of living lies in a fine mingling of letting go and holding on.
Havelock Ellis

Lulu Moonwood Murakami

assemblage: sewn, sculpted, painted, collage, fabric, paperclay, acrylic paint, wood, wire, paper

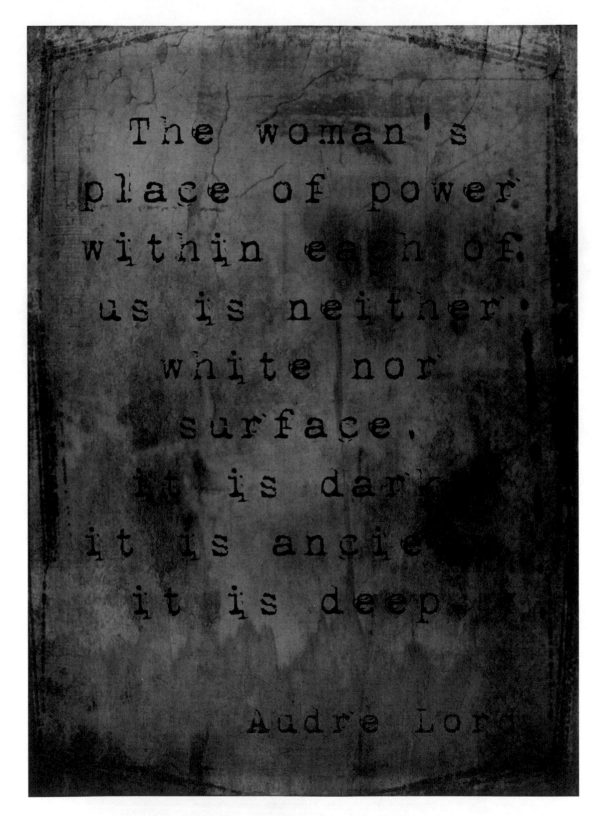

he woman's place of power within each of us is neither
white nor surface, it is dark, it is ancient, it is deep.
Audre Lord

NM Creatrix

digital collage

Above all, do not lose your desire to walk.
I have walked myself into the best thoughts.
Søren Kierkegaard

Diane Becka

fabric collage: fused appliqué, free motion embroidery, colored pencil

Look not too far afield...Answers lie within. What lies behind us and
what lies before us are tiny matters compared with what lies within.
Henry Stanley Haskins

Dayle Doroshow

stitched fabric collage

Ever try. Ever fail. No mattter.
Try again. Fail again. Fail better.
Samuel Beckett

Loretta Benedetto Marvel

lettering: pen, chalk, cardstock

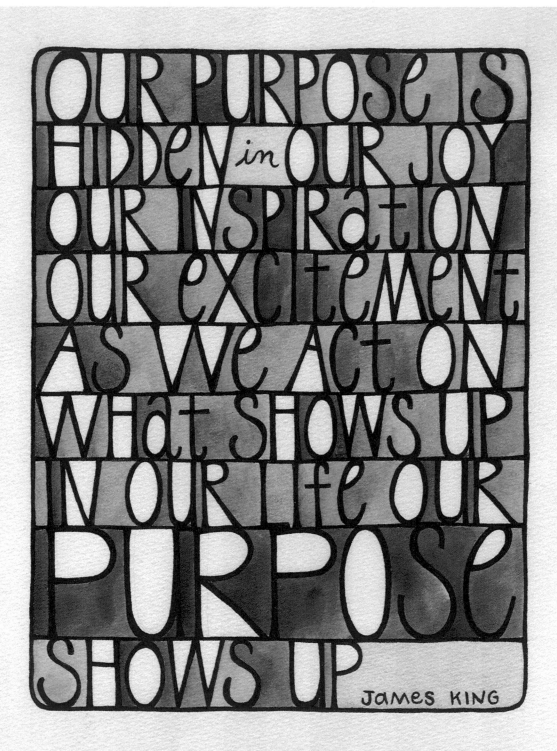

Our purpose is hidden in our joy, our inspiration, our excitement.
As we act on what shows up in our life, our pupose shows up.
James King

Pat Pitingolo

illustration: watercolor

There is no doing it right; there's just being with what is
as wholeheartedly as the moment allows.
Stephen Levine

Sheryl Eggleston

watercolor: paper collaged on painted canvas

There's a thread that binds all of us together; pull on
one end of the thread, the strain is felt all down the line.
Rosamond Marshall

Patti Edmon

mixed media collage

Time is not a line, but a series of now points.
Taisen Deshimaru

(Meg Greene)

digital collage: photograph

Your living is determined not so much by what life brings to you
as the attitude you bring to life.
John Home

Susan Hance

digital photograph

Your work is to discover your work and then
with all your heart to give yourself to it.
Buddha

Dayle Doroshow

fabric collage: transfer, stitching

I found I could say things with color and shapes that I
couldn't say any other way - things I had no words for.
Georgia O'Keefe

Adeola Davies-Aiyeloja

mixed media painting on board with acrylic skins

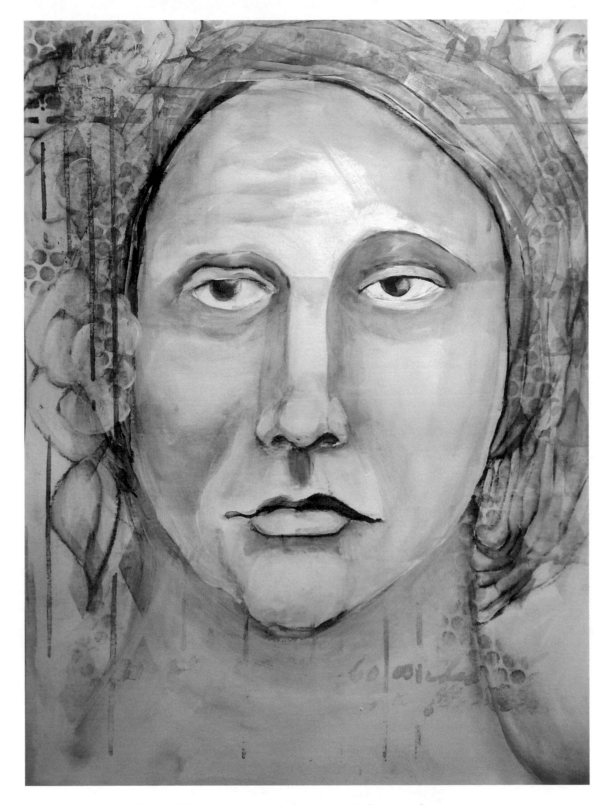

Beautiful young people are accidents of nature,
but beautiful old people are works of art.
Eleanor Roosevelt

Pam Carriker

layered painting: acrylics, graphite, water-soluble media

When you follow your bliss...doors will open where you would not have thought
there would be doors, and where there wouldn't be a door for anyone else.
Joseph Campbell

Jill Hejl

drawing & painting on watercolor paper

Why are you trying so hard to fit in when you were born to stand out.
Ian Wallace

Marla Jean Esser

recycled fence board assemblages: paint

People become really quite remarkable when they start thinking that they can do things.
When they believe in themselves they have the first secret of success.
Norman Vincent Peale

Lesley Riley

collage: Gelli plate prints on wood & fabric, TAP transfer on copper mesh

Cheryl Alt
Do It Now!
12" x 12"
Photo by Britni Wilson

Catherie Anderson
Inspiration Arriving
8" x10"
CatherineAndersonStudio.com

Seth Apter
Quite Still
5.5" x 7"
TheAlteredPage.blogspot.com

Gina Armfield
Untitled
9" x 12"
NoExcusesArt.com

Doris Arndt
Other Than Human
9" x 12"

Jan Avellana
I Would Still Plant My Apple Tree
8" x 10"
JanAvellana.com

Cheryl Bakke Martin
You Are What You Are When Nobody Is Looking
9" x 12"
inspirations-studio.com

Linda C. Bannan
Call It Joy
12" x 12"
Photo by Mike Bannan

Serena Barton
The Smallest Thing
6" x 6"
SerenaBarton.com

Diane Becka
The Walker
5" x 7"
DianeBecka.com

Marcia Beckett
We Are So Many Selves
8.5" x 11"
MarciaBeckett.blogspot.com

Jill K. Berry
Make It New
19" x 19"
JillBerryDesign.com

Darlene Campbell
Nothing Standard Here
Darlene-Freeniebelle.blogspot.com

Joyce L. Carrier
Autumn Paths
10" x 12.5"
CarrierClothworks.com

Pam Carriker
Youth Remembered
9" x 12"
PamCarriker.com

Lisa Chin
Grab Joy
20" x 14"
SomethingCleverAboutNothing.blogspot.com

Artist Directory

Carol Clarkson
Indian Chief
6" x 22"
Photo by Hunter Clarkson
CarolClarksonPottery.com

Judy Coates Perez
We Are Cups
12" x 15"
JudyCoatesPerez.com

Dawn Collins
Peace Art
9" x 12"
Meditating Girl
9" x 12"
ZetasAtticArt.blogspot.com

Tico
Subtle Blatancy
11" x 13.5"
Photo by Lisa Akers, Crawford Photography, LLC
KnitFunctionalFamily.blogspot.com

Sarah Cooper
Untitled
8.5" x 11.75" (Warhol)
11" x 8.5" (Bernhardt)
KeepsakesCrafts.blogspot.com

Chris Cozen
More is Hidden
5" x 7"
ChrisCozenArtist.typepad.com

Adeola Davies-Aiyeloja
Organic Red - Steps of Vision
14" x 14"
Green Mother Earth
8.5" x 11"
Facebook.com/AdeolaStudio

Holly Dean
Your World
10" x 10"
HollyDean.com

Ingrid Dijkers
The Heart That Breaks Open
9" x 15"
IngridDijkers.com

Dayle Doroshow
The Discovery
11" x 14"
My Inner Garden
11" x 14"
DayleDoroshow.com

Patti Edmon
Red Thread
8" x 8"
PattiEdmon.blogspot.com

Sheryl Eggleston
Pink Tree in Paradise
16" x 20"
SherylEggleston.blogspot.com

Marla Jean Esser
Expressions
Size Varies

Stephanie Estrin
Believe
11" x 14"
StephanieEstrin.blogspot.com

Jerry Gonzalez
A Quote by Jean-LucGoddard
8" x 10"
Jerrytoons.com

Meg Greene
Waiting with My Father for the Martins
6" x 10"
MoveTheChair.wordpress.com

Cheryl Greenstreet
Dusting
Photograph by William Johns

Paula Guerin
Untitled
8" x 10"
Life is a Spell
8" x 10"
Photo by Bernie Guerin
Etsy Shop - Luckduck

Deborah Guthrie
A Rainbow Gladdens My Heart
5" x 5"
My Imagination Flies When I Open a Book
5" x 5"

Susan E. Hance
Joy on Wheels
9" x 12"
SusanHance.com

Andrea Hawkes
'shroom
Photo by Murray Little

Jill Hejl
Follow Your Bliss
9" x 12"
livedrawpaint.blogspot.com

Sharon Hendry
You Become
7.5" x 8"
e14studio.blogspot.com

Lynne Hoppe
"t elf"
1.25" x 3"
LynneHoppe.blogspot.com

Lucy Pearce Hughes
Sunrise Serenity
14" x 11"
PearHugStudio.com

Barb Ingersoll
Change is in the Wind
10.125" x 12.875"

Jennifer Johns
Courage - Serenity Prayer Series
16" x 20"
jjohnsdesigns.com

"Lovey" Lavette Johnson-Debrow
When I Gaze Upon You
11.5" x 16"
fabricphotomemories.blogspot.com

Liz Kettle
The Journey is Easier with the Right Companions
11" x 14"

Ruth Krening
Untitled
7" x 8"
Photo by Nina Johnson

Mindy Lacefield
I Must Be a Mermaid
8" x 10"
TimsSally.com

Lucy Landry
Deep in the Garden of My Heart
7.5" x 15"
LucyLandryDesigns.com

Leslie Levenson
The History of the Mystery
8.5" x 11.7"
SteamingFork.com

Marlynn Likens
To Dream
8" x 10"
Photo by Trinh Hoang
HoneysuckleBreeze.blogspot.com

Gina Louthian-Stanley
Whispers of the Moon
6" x 6"
GinaLouthian-Stanley.blogspot.com

Sandy Lupton
Curious
7" x 13"
Luna
24" x 24"
shooting-star-gallery.com

Linda H. MacDonald
Wrong Tree
15" x 19"
macsplace.net/quilt.html

Catherine Martin
Oasis of Refreshment
10" x 13"

Theresa Martin
Here Comes the Sun
8" x 10"
teresamartin.com

Loretta Benedetto Marvel
Fail Better
8.5" x 11"
artjournaler.typepad.com/
pomegranatesandpaper

Stacey Merrill
Color the Sky
8" x 10"
Soaring
8" x 10"
artsnark.blogspot.com

Linda Teddlie Minton
Ring the Bells
8" x 10"
fiberreflections.blogspot.com

Susie Monday
When You Look at Art
16" x 24"
SusieMonday.com

Patti Monroe-Mohrenweiser
Spitirual Beings
8.5" x 10"
BeyondLetters.com

Pearl Red Moon
A Thread That Runs Through
21.5" x 25.5"
pearlredmoon.com

Lulu Moonwood Murakami
Letting Go & Holding On
20" x 16"
lulumoonart.com

NM Creatrix
Place of Power
8" x 11"
CreativityContinum.com

Norina Morris
Kindness
20" x 24"
Photo by Lesley Riley

Patricia J. Mosca
Feelings
5" x 7"
pjmosca.com

Karen O'Brien
The Color of Spring
6.5" x 9"
KarenOBrien.blogspot.com

Sue Bellone Perna
Moxie Metabolism
24" x 24"

Pat Pitingolo
Purpose
8" x 10"
PatPitingolo.blogspot.com

Lesley Riley
Secret of Success
8" x 10"
LesleyRiley.com

Jenny Rodda
Star Dreaming
8.5" x 11"

Sandra Ahlgren Sapienza
Judith
8" x 10"

Meena Schaldenbrand
Persistence!
22" x 30"
MeenaSchaldenbrand.blogspot.com

Tricia Scott
S.S. Unknown
20" x 20"
tricia-scott.com

Shimoda
I Found God
9.25" x 12"
Shimoda-Accessories.com

Carol Sloan
mixed media
10" x 8"
Photo by T.R. Sloan
CarolBSloan.blogspot.com

Bonnie J. Smith
Swimming Upstream
30" x 40"
Photo by Luke Mulks
BonnieJoFiberarts.com

Silvia Souza
Saint Emily
7" x 10"
PigsFlyStudio.com

Joanie Springer
Emily Hurries Home in Time for Tea
8" x 12"
ArtFortheSoulofIt.com

Cheryl Stevenson
Grace
9" x 12"
CherylStevenson.blogspot.com

Rachel Stewart
State of Mind
7.5" x 14"
Photo by Darren Lykes Photography
BlueFinchJewelry.blogspot.com

Theresa Wells Stifel
Untitled
16" x 20"
StifelandCapra.com

Vicki Szamborski
The Rose
11" x 14"
VickiInYourHead.wordpress.com

Kin Tedrow
Mary
8" x 10"
KimTedrow.blogspot.com

Liz Thoresen
The Ride of Your Life
9" x 12"
LizThoresen.com

Tamara Tolkin
Bury Doubt Under Wonder
8.5" x 14"

Michelle Tompkins
Beginning of a Beginning
24" x 36"
Photo by Russ Pace
VindicatedStudios.com

Larkin Jean Van Horn
The Muses Love the Morning
8.5" x 10.5"
Photo by G. Armour Van Horn
LarkinArt.com

Kirsten Varga
Sanctuary
8" x 10"
Destiny
7" x 9"
SmilingEyeStudio.blogspot.com

Kim Ward
Free Your Heart
4.75" diameter
KimMarieWard.blogspot.com

Ellen Wilson
Learning Curve
5" x 7"
Photo by Lesley Riley
EllasEdge.blogspot.com

Nanette S. Zeller
Courage
14" x 19"
NanetteSewz.com

Meet the Author

Lesley Riley wears many hats: she is an internationally known artist, quilter, teacher, writer, Artist Success coach and mentor, who turned her initial passion for photos, color and the written word into a dream *occupassion*.

Her art and articles have appeared in numerous publications and juried shows As former Contributing Editor of *Cloth Paper Scissors* magazine, Lesley showcased new talent in mixed media art. Her first book, *Quilted Memories*, brought new ideas and techniques to quilting and preserving memories, *Fabric Memory Books*, combined fabric and innovative ideas with the art of bookmaking. *Fabulous Fabric Art with Lutradur* and *Create with Transfer Artist Paper*, introduced versatile new materials to the mixed media art world. Her fifth book will debut summer 2014 from C&T Publishing.

Lesley introduced Transfer Artist Paper™, named CHA's 2011 Most Innovative new product, the state of the art technology for iron-on transfers.

Her passion and desire to help every artist reach their creative dreams and potential to has led a growing specialty as an Artist Success™ expert and coach, providing guidance and solutions for artists of all levels. To stay inspired and learn more about her online classes and in-person workshops and retreats, sign up for her bi-weekly dose of inspiration at LesleyRiley.com or ArtistSuccess.com.

Lesley's Favorite Quote Resources

~

ThinkExist.com
BrainyQuote.com
PaintersKeys.com

Copyright Free Image Sources

(all www.)

- e-vint.com
- nos.twnsnd.co (yes, dot co)
- vintageprintable.com
- loc.gov/pictures/
- digitalgallery.nypl.org
- graphicsfairy.com
- unprofound.com

Always be aware of and abide by any copyright restrictions on images you use in your artwork unless your use will always be strictly personal, for your eyes only.

Your Turn! Get Creative with QUOTES

Choose a quote from the book, one your favorites or one from my favorite websites.

How does this quote make you feel? Spend some time mulling this over.

What colors does it bring to mind?

What symbols, objects, images or photos from your past or present could you use to show and describe your feelings?

Gather some papers, glue, paint, markers and colored pencils. Using magazine images or your own items, create a collage that expresses the feelings and inspiration you get from the quote.

Consider keeping a personal journal of quotes that you find inspiring and motivating. Make it your private place to go wild with your thoughts, color, image and whatever moves you. I can tell you from experience that the more intimate and familiar you get with quotes, the more they can change your life...for the better. And you can quote me on that!

5117212R00062

Printed in Great Britain
by Amazon.co.uk, Ltd.,
Marston Gate.